JIU-JITSU

THE JOURNAL

柔術

THE JIU JITSU JOURNAL

A guided journal designed to help you learn effective tools for mastering jiu jitsu

. . . .
THIS BOOK BELONGS TO

. . . .
IF FOUND, PLEASE RETURN TO

The Jiu-Jitsu Journal
Published by Station 535

ISBN: 9781778007408
Printed in the United States of America

Author
Willow Seitz

Designed by
Willow Seitz

Edited by
Station 535

A Letter From The Author

Coming from a background of Yoshinkan Aikido, a somewhat controversial martial art in the Mixed Martial Arts community, I was taken aback by the competition in Jiu-Jitsu. Rolling, resisting, and actively fighting your partner's movements was a very unfamiliar concept to me. Aikido is the art of peace, and directly translates to "the way of harmony." I thought Jiu-Jitsu was the opposite of that due to its competitive nature.

Now that I've been training for a while, and after doing the research for this journal, I've realized that Aikido and Jiu-Jitsu are actually quite similar. The direct translation of jū into english is "gentle, soft, pliable, or yielding," and jutsu is "art or technique." Therefore, it can be translated as "yielding-art." The philosophy of this yielding art is to use the force of your opponent against them, to blend with their energy, rather than confronting it with your own.

Once I realized this, I fell in love, and committed myself to training. It's very difficult sometimes, currently being a 135lb female who is quite smaller and weaker than the rest of the people in my gym. But that's the beauty of this martial art. You don't need to be massive, or super strong, although those things do help. The biggest thing you need to be is intelligent. The only person you are truly in competition with is yourself. You have to work to be better than you were the day before; you must strive for perfection. Your opponent is not your enemy, your lack of knowledge and skills is.

My intention in creating this journal is to help you learn, memorize, and reflect your knowledge and skills in Jiu-Jitsu. You do not need to be a certain rank in Jiu-Jitsu to find this journal relevant or useful. Since this martial art is extremely technical and detail orientated, keeping a logbook of your training progress will help you remember more information and make progress. The idea is that you use this journal whenever you train, but there's no pressure. Many Jiu-Jitsu students keep journals but they don't always write in them after every class. Record and reflect on your experiences, thoughts, feelings and technique as often as you like.

This book is not magical—it will not suddenly make you amazing at the martial art—but it will help you direct your training in a way that makes sense to you, providing effective insights along the way. I will leave you with this note: believe in yourself, and be the harbinger of change in your body. I'll be cheering for you.

Sincerely,

Willow Seitz

Willow Seitz
2nd Degree Black Belt in Yoshinkan Aikido
Jujitsuka in Brazillian Jiu-Jitsu

Contents

Your Meal Planner

70% of your health and fitness relies on your diet. Choose meals that are beneficial to you and your personal training style. Feel free to use this space to keep track of what you are putting into your body.

MON

BREAKFAST LUNCH DINNER

TUE

BREAKFAST LUNCH DINNER

WED

BREAKFAST LUNCH DINNER

THU

BREAKFAST LUNCH DINNER

FRI

BREAKFAST LUNCH DINNER

SAT

BREAKFAST LUNCH DINNER

SUN

BREAKFAST LUNCH DINNER

Your Workout Planner

Jiu-Jitsu drives you to be flexible, strong, and have great
cardio. Many jujitsuka find it beneficial to excersise outside of class
to compliment their Jiu-Jitsu. You can use this space to
create your own workout schedule that fits your individual needs.

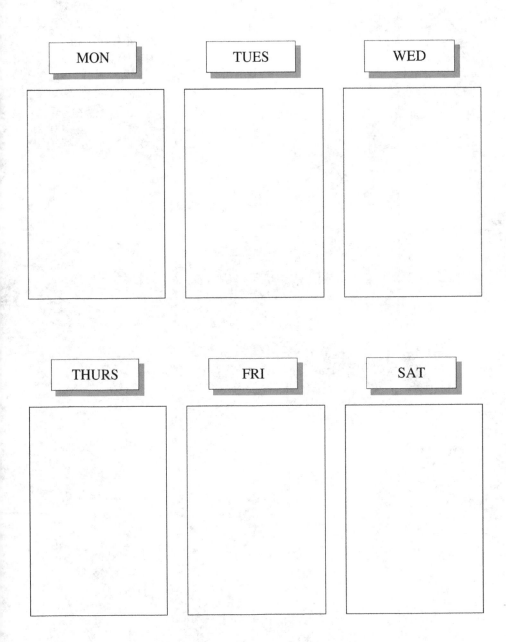

MON

TUES

WED

THURS

FRI

SAT

1 INTRODUCTION:
Goals and Intentions

1.   Setting a specific intention can help guide you on your Jiu-Jitsu
      journey. What purpose do you hope this logbook will serve?
      What purpose do you hope to get out of using it? Be as factual or
      abstract as feels right.

2.   What are the major anxieties or struggles you are currently facing
      in Jiu Jitsu? List any or all of that you would like to address with
      this journal.

Your Journal Entries

1.   How are you feeling right now?   (Tune in with yourself)

2.   What techniques did you practice?   (Keep it simple)

3.   What were your successes?   (Note what you did well)

1.   What do you need to work on?   (Be specific)

2.   Did you meet your goals?   (What did you meet or not meet?)

3.   What are your goals for next class?   (Note what you did well)

NOTE FROM A JUJITSUKA — Carlos Gracie, Sr.

There is no losing in jiu jitsu. You either win or you learn.

1. How are you feeling right now? (Tune in with yourself)

2. What techniques did you practice? (Keep it simple)

3. What were your successes? (Note what you did well)

1.   What do you need to work on?   (Be specific)

2.   Did you meet your goals?   (What did you meet or not meet?)

3.   What are your goals for next class?   (Note what you did well)

A NOTE FROM A JUJITSUKA — Renzo Gracie

My opponent is my teacher, my ego is my enemy.

1.   How are you feeling right now?   (Tune in with yourself)

2.   What techniques did you practice?   (Keep it simple)

3.   What were your successes?   (Note what you did well)

1.   What do you need to work on?   (Be specific)

2.   Did you meet your goals?   (What did you meet or not meet?)

3.   What are your goals for next class?   (Note what you did well)

A NOTE FROM A JUJITSUKA — Helio Gracie

Always assume that your opponent is going to be bigger, stronger and faster than you; so that you learn to rely on technique, timing and leverage rather than brute strength.

1.   How are you feeling right now?   (Tune in with yourself)

2.   What techniques did you practice?   (Keep it simple)

3.   What were your successes?   (Note what you did well)

1.   What do you need to work on?   (Be specific)

2.   Did you meet your goals?   (What did you meet or not meet?)

3.   What are your goals for next class?   (Note what you did well)

A NOTE FROM A JUJITSUKA — Carlson Gracie, Sr.

If you want to be a lion, you must train with lions.

1.   How are you feeling right now?   (Tune in with yourself)

2.   What techniques did you practice?   (Keep it simple)

3.   What were your successes?   (Note what you did well)

1.   What do you need to work on?   (Be specific)

2.   Did you meet your goals?   (What did you meet or not meet?)

3.   What are your goals for next class?   (Note what you did well)

A NOTE FROM A JUJITSUKA — Rickson Gracie

Jiu Jitsu is perfect. It's humans who make errors.

1.   How are you feeling right now?   (Tune in with yourself)

2.   What techniques did you practice?   (Keep it simple)

3.   What were your successes?   (Note what you did well)

1. What do you need to work on? (Be specific)

2. Did you meet your goals? (What did you meet or not meet?)

3. What are your goals for next class? (Note what you did well)

A NOTE FROM A JUJITSUKA — Carlos Gracie

The biggest lesson I learned from jiu-jitsu was how to truly know myself.

1.   How are you feeling right now?   (Tune in with yourself)

2.   What techniques did you practice?   (Keep it simple)

3.   What were your successes?   (Note what you did well)

1. What do you need to work on? (Be specific)

2. Did you meet your goals? (What did you meet or not meet?)

3. What are your goals for next class? (Note what you did well)

A NOTE FROM A JUJITSUKA — Joe Rogan

If you want to learn technique, learn Jiu Jitsu. Learn from a light guy. Learn from a guy who had to struggle and really learn how to do it correctly.

1.   How are you feeling right now?   (Tune in with yourself)

2.   What techniques did you practice?   (Keep it simple)

3.   What were your successes?   (Note what you did well)

1.   What do you need to work on?   (Be specific)

2.   Did you meet your goals?   (What did you meet or not meet?)

3.   What are your goals for next class?   (Note what you did well)

A NOTE FROM A JUJITSUKA — Royce Gracie

Jiu-Jitsu is not the art of hitting, it's the art of not getting hit.

1.   How are you feeling right now?   (Tune in with yourself)

2.   What techniques did you practice?   (Keep it simple)

3.   What were your successes?   (Note what you did well)

1.   What do you need to work on?   (Be specific)

2.   Did you meet your goals?   (What did you meet or not meet?)

3.   What are your goals for next class?   (Note what you did well)

A NOTE FROM A JUJITSUKA — Saulo Ribeiro

If you think, you are late. If you are late, you use strength. If you use strength, you tire. And if you tire, you die.

1.   How are you feeling right now?   (Tune in with yourself)

2.   What techniques did you practice?   (Keep it simple)

3.   What were your successes?   (Note what you did well)

1.   What do you need to work on?   (Be specific)

2.   Did you meet your goals?   (What did you meet or not meet?)

3.   What are your goals for next class?   (Note what you did well)

A NOTE FROM A JUJITSUKA — Saulo Ribeiro

Just as the child must trust his mother, the white belt must believe in the good will of his instructor. There will be a time for questioning, but for now he must focus and train.

1. Check-In

1. Look through your last section of journal entries for patterns. Are there certain thoughts, feelings, successes or problems that are more frequent?

2. What approaches to improving are working the best?

3. What's one thing you can do differently for the next section of journal entries?

1.   How are you feeling right now?   (Tune in with yourself)

2.   What techniques did you practice?   (Keep it simple)

3.   What were your successes?   (Note what you did well)

1.   What do you need to work on?   (Be specific)

2.   Did you meet your goals?   (What did you meet or not meet?)

3.   What are your goals for next class?   (Note what you did well)

A NOTE FROM A JUJITSUKA — Saulo Ribeiro

When you react, you don't give your mind the time to get filled with emotions. You are devoid of anger, fear, and frustration; you are simply moving.

1.   How are you feeling right now?   (Tune in with yourself)

2.   What techniques did you practice?   (Keep it simple)

3.   What were your successes?   (Note what you did well)

1.   What do you need to work on?   (Be specific)

2.   Did you meet your goals?   (What did you meet or not meet?)

3.   What are your goals for next class?   (Note what you did well)

A NOTE FROM A JUJITSUKA — Mark Johnson

A balanced game will allow you to attack from both sides, making your skills more complete, more effective, and essentially doubling your techniques. Always drill both sides. Balance is good.

1.   How are you feeling right now?   (Tune in with yourself)

2.   What techniques did you practice?   (Keep it simple)

3.   What were your successes?   (Note what you did well)

1.   What do you need to work on?   (Be specific)

2.   Did you meet your goals?   (What did you meet or not meet?)

3.   What are your goals for next class?   (Note what you did well)

A NOTE FROM A JUJITSUKA — Rodolfo Vieira

To be good at Jiu-Jitsu it's all about believing and training, there isn't that much else you can do.

1.   How are you feeling right now?   (Tune in with yourself)

2.   What techniques did you practice?   (Keep it simple)

3.   What were your successes?   (Note what you did well)

1.   What do you need to work on?   (Be specific)

2.   Did you meet your goals?   (What did you meet or not meet?)

3.   What are your goals for next class?   (Note what you did well)

A NOTE FROM A JUJITSUKA — Ryron Gracie

Spend more time in a Jiu-Jitsu gi than in street clothes.

1.   How are you feeling right now?   (Tune in with yourself)

2.   What techniques did you practice?   (Keep it simple)

3.   What were your successes?   (Note what you did well)

1.   What do you need to work on?   (Be specific)

2.   Did you meet your goals?   (What did you meet or not meet?)

3.   What are your goals for next class?   (Note what you did well)

A NOTE FROM A JUJITSUKA — Ryron Gracie

I do Jiu-Jitsu so I can protect you when I fight you.

1.   How are you feeling right now?   (Tune in with yourself)

2.   What techniques did you practice?   (Keep it simple)

3.   What were your successes?   (Note what you did well)

1.   What do you need to work on?   (Be specific)

2.   Did you meet your goals?   (What did you meet or not meet?)

3.   What are your goals for next class?   (Note what you did well)

A NOTE FROM A JUJITSUKA — Rillion Gracie

Learning defense improves the attack. If the lion knows how the prey can escape, it'll capture it in a much more precise way.

1.   How are you feeling right now?   (Tune in with yourself)

2.   What techniques did you practice?   (Keep it simple)

3.   What were your successes?   (Note what you did well)

1.　　　What do you need to work on?　　　　　　　　　　　　(Be specific)

2.　　　Did you meet your goals?　　　　　　　　　(What did you meet or not meet?)

3.　　　What are your goals for next class?　　　　　　(Note what you did well)

A NOTE FROM A JUJITSUKA — Chris Matakas

After I received my blue belt, I soon recognized that the belts were simply an external representation of an inner experience, and that they mattered little compared to the person I was becoming.

1.   How are you feeling right now?   (Tune in with yourself)

2.   What techniques did you practice?   (Keep it simple)

3.   What were your successes?   (Note what you did well)

1.   What do you need to work on?   (Be specific)

2.   Did you meet your goals?   (What did you meet or not meet?)

3.   What are your goals for next class?   (Note what you did well)

A NOTE FROM A JUJITSUKA — Chris Matakas

We can lose the roll, we can lose position, but we can constantly strive to win the moment.

1.   How are you feeling right now?   (Tune in with yourself)

2.   What techniques did you practice?   (Keep it simple)

3.   What were your successes?   (Note what you did well)

1.   What do you need to work on?   (Be specific)

2.   Did you meet your goals?   (What did you meet or not meet?)

3.   What are your goals for next class?   (Note what you did well)

A NOTE FROM A JUJITSUKA — Rickson Gracie

The evolutionary process in jiu-jitsu makes you feel everytime more capable to see the underlines, to anticipate the move, to become better connected with the elements no matter if it's physical, spiritual or mental.

1.   How are you feeling right now?   (Tune in with yourself)

2.   What techniques did you practice?   (Keep it simple)

3.   What were your successes?   (Note what you did well)

1.   What do you need to work on?   (Be specific)

2.   Did you meet your goals?   (What did you meet or not meet?)

3.   What are your goals for next class?   (Note what you did well)

A NOTE FROM A JUJITSUKA — John Danaher

Anger just makes people inefficient. Their breathing gets shallow, they're too muscularly tense; they gas faster.

2. Check-In

1. Look through your last section of journal entries for patterns. Are there certain thoughts, feelings, successes or problems that are more frequent?

2. What approaches to improving are working the best?

3. What's one thing you can do differently for the next section of journal entries?

1.   How are you feeling right now?   (Tune in with yourself)

2.   What techniques did you practice?   (Keep it simple)

3.   What were your successes?   (Note what you did well)

1.   What do you need to work on?   (Be specific)

2.   Did you meet your goals?   (What did you meet or not meet?)

3.   What are your goals for next class?   (Note what you did well)

A NOTE FROM A JUJITSUKA — Saulo Ribeiro

When I see you grapple, I am not impressed if you win or lose. What I want to see is your use of the fundamentals of jiu-jitsu. It does not matter how it ends. I do not care if you tap five times as long as you try to use technique.

1.　　　How are you feeling right now?　　　　　　　　(Tune in with yourself)

2.　　　What techniques did you practice?　　　　　　　　(Keep it simple)

3.　　　What were your successes?　　　　　　　　(Note what you did well)

1.   What do you need to work on?   (Be specific)

2.   Did you meet your goals?   (What did you meet or not meet?)

3.   What are your goals for next class?   (Note what you did well)

A NOTE FROM A JUJITSUKA — Renzo Gracie

For me the white belt is the most precious asset we have. This is the people we have to take care of, we have to look over them, we have to make sure they learn right and get better.

1.   How are you feeling right now?   (Tune in with yourself)

2.   What techniques did you practice?   (Keep it simple)

3.   What were your successes?   (Note what you did well)

1.   What do you need to work on?   (Be specific)

2.   Did you meet your goals?   (What did you meet or not meet?)

3.   What are your goals for next class?   (Note what you did well)

A NOTE FROM A JUJITSUKA — Marcelo Garcia

Everyone is the same for the first two minutes, everyone has a chance to win, but after that, you start to separate physically and mentally.

1.　　How are you feeling right now?　　　　　　　　　　(Tune in with yourself)

2.　　What techniques did you practice?　　　　　　　　　　(Keep it simple)

3.　　What were your successes?　　　　　　　　　　(Note what you did well)

1.   What do you need to work on?   (Be specific)

2.   Did you meet your goals?   (What did you meet or not meet?)

3.   What are your goals for next class?   (Note what you did well)

A NOTE FROM A JUJITSUKA — Rickson Gracie

The most interesting aspect of jiu-jit-su is… of course the techniques are great…but the sensibility of the opponent, sense of touch, the weight, the momentum, the transition from one movement to another. That's the amazing thing about it. You must allow yourself to go as on autopilot.

1. How are you feeling right now? (Tune in with yourself)

2. What techniques did you practice? (Keep it simple)

3. What were your successes? (Note what you did well)

1.   What do you need to work on?   (Be specific)

2.   Did you meet your goals?   (What did you meet or not meet?)

3.   What are your goals for next class?   (Note what you did well)

A NOTE FROM A JUJITSUKA — Pedro Sauer

If you attach to each other, and hold each other very tight what happens is neither of you move. Nothing happens in the training. That's not Gracie Jiu-jitsu. The real Gracie Jiu-jitsu – you don't hold tight, you hold the opponent with open hands. You let him move and after that you counter him. It is 100% counterattacks.

1.   How are you feeling right now?   (Tune in with yourself)

2.   What techniques did you practice?   (Keep it simple)

3.   What were your successes?   (Note what you did well)

1.   What do you need to work on?   (Be specific)

2.   Did you meet your goals?   (What did you meet or not meet?)

3.   What are your goals for next class?   (Note what you did well)

A NOTE FROM A JUJITSUKA — Roger Gracie

Use your own weight to crush your opponent.

1.   How are you feeling right now?   (Tune in with yourself)

2.   What techniques did you practice?   (Keep it simple)

3.   What were your successes?   (Note what you did well)

1.   What do you need to work on?   (Be specific)

2.   Did you meet your goals?   (What did you meet or not meet?)

3.   What are your goals for next class?   (Note what you did well)

A NOTE FROM A JUJITSUKA — Helio Gracie

I do not defeat my opponents, they defeat themselves.

1.   How are you feeling right now?   (Tune in with yourself)

2.   What techniques did you practice?   (Keep it simple)

3.   What were your successes?   (Note what you did well)

1. What do you need to work on? (Be specific)

2. Did you meet your goals? (What did you meet or not meet?)

3. What are your goals for next class? (Note what you did well)

A NOTE FROM A JUJITSUKA — Carlson Gracie Sr.

Always enter like a kitten and leave like a lion. But never enter like a lion and leave like a kitten. Always be humble.

1.   How are you feeling right now?   (Tune in with yourself)

2.   What techniques did you practice?   (Keep it simple)

3.   What were your successes?   (Note what you did well)

1.   What do you need to work on?   (Be specific)

2.   Did you meet your goals?   (What did you meet or not meet?)

3.   What are your goals for next class?   (Note what you did well)

A NOTE FROM A JUJITSUKA — Rickson Gracie

Even when you spar during training, you should minimize your natural talents.

By limiting yourself, you may find yourself in much worse situation, but you are forced to think your way out.

1.   How are you feeling right now?   (Tune in with yourself)

2.   What techniques did you practice?   (Keep it simple)

3.   What were your successes?   (Note what you did well)

1.   What do you need to work on?   (Be specific)

2.   Did you meet your goals?   (What did you meet or not meet?)

3.   What are your goals for next class?   (Note what you did well)

A NOTE FROM A JUJITSUKA — Rafa Mendes

Athletes are not permitted certain luxuries like drinking, partying, and eating whatever they want.

3. Check-In

1. Look through your last section of journal entries for patterns. Are there certain thoughts, feelings, successes or problems that are more frequent?

2. What approaches to improving are working the best?

3. What's one thing you can do differently for the next section of journal entries?

1.   How are you feeling right now?   (Tune in with yourself)

2.   What techniques did you practice?   (Keep it simple)

3.   What were your successes?   (Note what you did well)

1.   What do you need to work on?   (Be specific)

2.   Did you meet your goals?   (What did you meet or not meet?)

3.   What are your goals for next class?   (Note what you did well)

A NOTE FROM A JUJITSUKA — Miyamoto Musashi

Today is victory over yourself of yesterday; tomorrow is your victory over lesser men.

1.   How are you feeling right now?   (Tune in with yourself)

2.   What techniques did you practice?   (Keep it simple)

3.   What were your successes?   (Note what you did well)

1.   What do you need to work on?   (Be specific)

2.   Did you meet your goals?   (What did you meet or not meet?)

3.   What are your goals for next class?   (Note what you did well)

A NOTE FROM A JUJITSUKA — Carlos Gracie Jr.

I've always been a fan of the basics. After you have a good solid foundation of Jiu-Jitsu, the rest comes by instinct. You create, invent. The rest is easy. The difficult part is the beginning.

1.   How are you feeling right now?   (Tune in with yourself)

2.   What techniques did you practice?   (Keep it simple)

3.   What were your successes?   (Note what you did well)

1.   What do you need to work on?   (Be specific)

2.   Did you meet your goals?   (What did you meet or not meet?)

3.   What are your goals for next class?   (Note what you did well)

A NOTE FROM A JUJITSUKA — Sam Harris

To train in Jiu-Jitsu is to continually drown—or, rather, to be drowned, in sudden and ingenious ways—and to be taught, again and again, how to swim.

1.   How are you feeling right now?   (Tune in with yourself)

2.   What techniques did you practice?   (Keep it simple)

3.   What were your successes?   (Note what you did well)

1.   What do you need to work on?   (Be specific)

2.   Did you meet your goals?   (What did you meet or not meet?)

3.   What are your goals for next class?   (Note what you did well)

A NOTE FROM A JUJITSUKA — Marcelo Garcia

I always want to be in the top position. Always. My entire game is built around sweeping my opponent and getting on top where I can use agility, positioning, and gravity to overwhelm my opponent's defences.

1.   How are you feeling right now?   (Tune in with yourself)

2.   What techniques did you practice?   (Keep it simple)

3.   What were your successes?   (Note what you did well)

1.   What do you need to work on?   (Be specific)

2.   Did you meet your goals?   (What did you meet or not meet?)

3.   What are your goals for next class?   (Note what you did well)

A NOTE FROM A JUJITSUKA — John Danaher

Learning how to learn is absolutely one of the keys to success in life in general and sport Jiu Jitsu in particular.

1.   How are you feeling right now?   (Tune in with yourself)

2.   What techniques did you practice?   (Keep it simple)

3.   What were your successes?   (Note what you did well)

1.   What do you need to work on?   (Be specific)

2.   Did you meet your goals?   (What did you meet or not meet?)

3.   What are your goals for next class?   (Note what you did well)

A NOTE FROM A JUJITSUKA — Gordon Ryan

The more time you spend fighting out of bad positions in training, the more confident you become in your defense. The more confident in your defense, the more confident you will be in attacking your opponent knowing that if you end up in a bad position, you can easily recover.

1.   How are you feeling right now?   (Tune in with yourself)

2.   What techniques did you practice?   (Keep it simple)

3.   What were your successes?   (Note what you did well)

1.   What do you need to work on?   (Be specific)

2.   Did you meet your goals?   (What did you meet or not meet?)

3.   What are your goals for next class?   (Note what you did well)

A NOTE FROM A JUJITSUKA — Keenan Cornelius

I've drilled them so many times, my body just reacts now. I can go out and let instinct take over.

1.   How are you feeling right now?   (Tune in with yourself)

2.   What techniques did you practice?   (Keep it simple)

3.   What were your successes?   (Note what you did well)

1.   What do you need to work on?   (Be specific)

2.   Did you meet your goals?   (What did you meet or not meet?)

3.   What are your goals for next class?   (Note what you did well)

A NOTE FROM A JUJITSUKA — Rorion Gracie

The most significant victories are the ones we accomplish within ourselves.

1. How are you feeling right now? (Tune in with yourself)

2. What techniques did you practice? (Keep it simple)

3. What were your successes? (Note what you did well)

1.   What do you need to work on?   (Be specific)

2.   Did you meet your goals?   (What did you meet or not meet?)

3.   What are your goals for next class?   (Note what you did well)

A NOTE FROM A JUJITSUKA — Royce Gracie

A black belt only covers two inches of your body. You have to cover the rest.

1.   How are you feeling right now?   (Tune in with yourself)

2.   What techniques did you practice?   (Keep it simple)

3.   What were your successes?   (Note what you did well)

1.   What do you need to work on?   (Be specific)

2.   Did you meet your goals?   (What did you meet or not meet?)

3.   What are your goals for next class?   (Note what you did well)

A NOTE FROM A JUJITSUKA — Kano Jigoro

The pine fought the storm and broke. The willow yielded to the wind and snow and did not break. Practice Jiu-Jitsu in just this way.

4. Check-In

1. Look through your last section of journal entries for patterns. Are there certain thoughts, feelings, successes or problems that are more frequent?

2. What approaches to improving are working the best?

3. What's one thing you can do differently for the next section of journal entries?

1.   How are you feeling right now?   (Tune in with yourself)

2.   What techniques did you practice?   (Keep it simple)

3.   What were your successes?   (Note what you did well)

1.　　　What do you need to work on?　　　　　　　　　　　　　　(Be specific)

2.　　　Did you meet your goals?　　　　　　　　(What did you meet or not meet?)

3.　　　What are your goals for next class?　　　　　　　(Note what you did well)

A NOTE FROM A JUJITSUKA — Rener Gracie

When you do Jiu-Jitsu, you won't look at a bigger guy and say oh no, you'll look and say how interesting!

1. How are you feeling right now? (Tune in with yourself)

2. What techniques did you practice? (Keep it simple)

3. What were your successes? (Note what you did well)

1.   What do you need to work on?   (Be specific)

2.   Did you meet your goals?   (What did you meet or not meet?)

3.   What are your goals for next class?   (Note what you did well)

A NOTE FROM A JUJITSUKA — Rickson Gracie

You can not anticipate what is going to happen. You must allow yourself to be in a zero point; a neutral point. Be relaxed and connected with the variations.

1.   How are you feeling right now?   (Tune in with yourself)

2.   What techniques did you practice?   (Keep it simple)

3.   What were your successes?   (Note what you did well)

1.   What do you need to work on?   (Be specific)

2.   Did you meet your goals?   (What did you meet or not meet?)

3.   What are your goals for next class?   (Note what you did well)

A NOTE FROM A JUJITSUKA — Leo Vieira

A champion should ask himself: if I were to compete against myself, what would I practice to beat me?

1.   How are you feeling right now?   (Tune in with yourself)

2.   What techniques did you practice?   (Keep it simple)

3.   What were your successes?   (Note what you did well)

1.   What do you need to work on?   (Be specific)

2.   Did you meet your goals?   (What did you meet or not meet?)

3.   What are your goals for next class?   (Note what you did well)

A NOTE FROM A JUJITSUKA — Saulo Ribeiro

Jiu-jitsu is the gentle art. It's the art where a small man or woman is going to prove to you, no matter how strong you are, no matter how mad you get, that you're going to have to accept defeat.

1.   How are you feeling right now?   (Tune in with yourself)

2.   What techniques did you practice?   (Keep it simple)

3.   What were your successes?   (Note what you did well)

1.   What do you need to work on?   (Be specific)

2.   Did you meet your goals?   (What did you meet or not meet?)

3.   What are your goals for next class?   (Note what you did well)

A NOTE FROM A JUJITSUKA — Keenan Cornelius

Before a big tournament, I stick to the stuff I've been doing and just drill it to death. If you're thinking about what to do next, your competitor is already moving to his next move. It's best to just react and let your body take over.

1.   How are you feeling right now?   (Tune in with yourself)

2.   What techniques did you practice?   (Keep it simple)

3.   What were your successes?   (Note what you did well)

1.   What do you need to work on?   (Be specific)

2.   Did you meet your goals?   (What did you meet or not meet?)

3.   What are your goals for next class?   (Note what you did well)

A NOTE FROM A JUJITSUKA — U.S. President Teddy Roosevelt

The art of Jiu-Jitsu is worth more in every way than all of our athletics combined.

1.   How are you feeling right now?   (Tune in with yourself)

2.   What techniques did you practice?   (Keep it simple)

3.   What were your successes?   (Note what you did well)

1.   What do you need to work on?   (Be specific)

2.   Did you meet your goals?   (What did you meet or not meet?)

3.   What are your goals for next class?   (Note what you did well)

A NOTE FROM A JUJITSUKA — Jean Jacques Machado

If you ask me what belt I am today, I'll tell you that I'm a white belt that never gave up.

Notes